QUESTIONS AND ANSWERS ABOUT WEATHER

by M. J. CRAIG ■ illustrated by LEN EBERT

SCHOLASTIC INC.

NEW YORK   TORONTO   LONDON   AUCKLAND   SYDNEY

CONTENTS

HURRICANES AND BREEZES

WHAT A CLOUDY, GRAY DAY!

FLASH AND CRASH

YOU AND I AND THE WEATHER FORECASTER

IT ALL BEGINS WITH THE SUN

Every kind of weather in the world is made by the sun.

Whenever the strong, bright light of the sun shines straight down through the air and against the earth, the earth grows warm. The air above the earth grows warm. Then we have warm weather, because of the sun.

Sometimes, of course, the weather is cold. Wherever the sun's light slants through the air and across the earth, the earth is colder, and the air above the earth is colder. Then the weather is colder. So we have colder weather, too, because of the sun.

Is windy weather caused by the sun? Yes, it is. Wind is cool air moving toward warmer air. Or sometimes it is warm air moving toward cooler air. And air is warm or cool because of the sun. So even windy weather begins with the sun.

Sometimes the weather is gray and cloudy. Sometimes it rains, or snows. It is the sun's heat that makes water vapor rise up from the earth to form clouds. And it is cooler air that makes the clouds drop rain, or snow, down to the earth again. You could really say that you put on a raincoat or build a snowman because of the sun.

Warm or cold, wet or dry, windy or still, bright or gray — all of the world's weather begins with the sun.

THE SEASONS AND THE SUN

Why is it warm in the summer and cold in the winter? Why do we have seasons?

It takes a year for the earth to travel in a big circle around the sun. As it moves, it is always tipped to one side a little.

Some of the year, the part of the earth where we live tips toward the sun. The sunlight shines straight down on it, and we have summer weather.

Some of the year, the part of the earth where we live leans away from the sun. The sunlight slants across it, and so we have winter weather. Another reason it is colder in winter is that winter days are shorter than summer days. There are not so many hours of sunshine each day to warm the earth.

Spring and fall are in-between kinds of seasons. In the spring the weather is changing from winter-cold to summer-warm. In the fall the weather is on its way from warm back to cold again.

Why doesn't it ever get cold near the equator?

Near the equator the sun shines almost straight down on the earth all year long, so the earth and the air stay warm all the time.

Why is it very hot one summer and cooler another summer? Why does spring come late some years? Why are some winters not very cold at all?

People have wondered for thousands of years why the seasons of one year were not exactly the same as the seasons of another year.

Now we have learned that the thin air several miles above the earth is full of great winds and storms and other movements. These winds are so high above the earth that we can't feel them. We don't know very much about them yet, but we do know that they have something to do with making our seasons different in different years.

Why is the sun so hot?

It is made of gas that is burning very fiercely.

How hot is the sun?

The surface of the sun is blazing away at about 10,000 degrees Fahrenheit. (When the temperature on earth is only about 90 to 95 degrees, that is what we call a blazing hot day.)
The inside of the sun, scientists think, is even hotter than the outside. It may have a temperature of over 30 million degrees!

Will the sun ever cool down?

Yes, but not for millions and millions and millions of years.

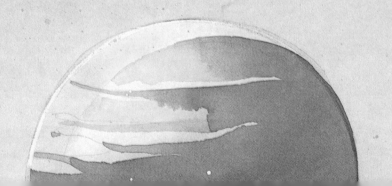

Does the sun spin around like a top, the way the earth does?

It does, but much more slowly. The earth spins all the way around once every day. But the sun takes more than three weeks to spin around just once.

What are sunspots?

They are large dark spots on the sun. They may come from explosions of gas deep inside the sun, but no one is sure.

Sunspots appear for a few days at a time. Sometimes they last for two or three weeks before they die away again. Once in a long while they last for several months.

Scientists have been trying to find out if sunspots make our weather change.

Why does the sky look blue when the sun is shining?

We call ordinary sunlight white light, because we cannot see any color in it. But sunlight is really a mixture of many different colors of light.

The sunlight that reaches us passes through air and dust high above the earth. Some of the blue rays of the sunlight make the air and the dust look blue. When we look at a clear blue sky, what we really see are very tiny bits of air and very tiny specks of dust glowing with a blue light.

HOT, COLD, AND IN BETWEEN

When was the hottest summer day in the United States?

On July 10, 1913, the temperature in Death Valley, California, was 134 degrees Fahrenheit. That was more than eighty years ago, but we haven't had a hotter day in the United States since then.

How cold can it be outdoors?

It was almost 129 degrees below zero Fahrenheit (−128.6° F.) at Vostok Station in Antarctica on July 21, 1983. Perhaps it has been even colder some other place or some other time, but no one was there with a thermometer to make sure.

Why is the beach cooler than the country or the city?

In the summer, the air over the sea is usually cooler than the air over the land. As the warm air over the land rises, the cooler air over the ocean keeps moving in toward the beach to take its place. This is called a sea breeze, and it feels just fine on a hot summer afternoon.

Why is the weather cool in the morning and warm later in the day?

Wherever it is night on earth, that part of the earth cools off. The warm sun is not shining on it. After the sun comes up in the morning, the earth gets warmer and warmer during the day. The middle of the afternoon, when the sun has been shining for many hours, is usually the warmest time of the day.

Why is it cold inside a deep cave?

That's very easy to answer if you think for a minute. How much sunlight can get inside a deep cave to warm it up?

How does a thermometer work?

A thermometer is used to measure the temperature of the air around it or anything else that touches it.

To make a thermometer, a very narrow glass tube is partly filled with liquid. Sometimes the liquid is silvery mercury; sometimes it is alcohol, colored red so you can see it easily. The air in the rest of the tube is pulled out, and the tube is sealed off at both ends. (The space left at the top where the air *was* is called a vacuum.)

When the tube is warmed, then the liquid inside gets warm too. When the liquid gets warm, it takes up more space. There is no place for the liquid to go but up, so it rises in the tube. When the tube and the liquid are cooled, the liquid shrinks. It takes up less room in the tube. It goes down again.

The tube is marked with lines to show exact degrees of temperature.

HURRICANES AND BREEZES

What makes wind blow? How does it start blowing?

Sometimes the air in one place is warmer than the air in another place near it. Warm air is thinner and lighter than cool air.

When heavier cool air touches warm air, it presses against it and pushes. Some of the warm air moves sideways, and some of it moves up. As the warm air keeps moving to the side and up and out of the way, the cool air flows in to take its place. This movement of the air is the wind.

Most of the air all over the surface of the earth is moving, a little or a lot, most of the time. We live on a windy world.

When you run, why is there wind on your face even if the wind isn't blowing?

Rub your finger against your nose. Now rub your nose against your finger. Either way, it feels just the same to your nose, doesn't it?

When the wind blows, air moves past your face.

When you run, your face moves past air. Either way, it feels just the same to your face.
Doesn't it?

When do we call a strong wind a hurricane?

The United States Weather Bureau calls a wind a hurricane when it blows as fast as 74 miles an hour.

What makes a hurricane stop?

A hurricane spins very fast when it moves across warm water, but it slows down and dies away if its path takes it over land. A hurricane that turns out to sea will die out when it reaches colder water or cooler air.

Are there ever any hurricanes where I live?

Where *do* you live? Most of our hurricanes start over the Atlantic Ocean or the Caribbean Sea, south of the United States, and blow toward the north. Some of them turn toward the Gulf of Mexico; some of them travel up the eastern coast. If you live near the south or east coasts of the United States, you might have been in a hurricane. If you live in another part of the country, you are not likely to be in a hurricane. You might have other kinds of bad storms, though, such as tornadoes.

What is a tornado?

A tornado is a windstorm that begins over land. Sometimes cold dry air blows very hard, and in a special way, against very warm wet air. When the two kinds of air meet, they often form a very large thunderstorm. The air beneath the storm begins to twist around. It spins faster and faster — perhaps as fast as 500 miles an hour.

The spinning air may take the shape of a funnel, and then move across the surface of the earth, still spinning.

The path of a tornado is often only as wide as a city block. (A hurricane can be over 500 miles wide.) A tornado does not last as long as a hurricane does, or travel as far. But wherever that spinning funnel of air touches the earth, it can cause a great deal of damage.

WHAT A CLOUDY, GRAY DAY!

What is water vapor?

Water is a liquid, but water vapor is not a liquid. It is a gas. Water vapor is bits of water so tiny that you can not see them. All of the air near the earth has some water vapor mixed with it.

Where does water vapor come from?

Tiny bits of water vapor float off into the air from anything at all that is wet — a puddle, a lake, a river, an ocean, a leaf on a tree, your skin, your breath. Water vapor comes from anything that is even the least bit damp.

What are clouds made of?

When water vapor rises from the earth, it cools. When it cools, the tiny bits of water come together and form small water droplets. Clouds are made of these water droplets, and sometimes of very tiny specks of ice too.

Water droplets are much bigger than bits of water vapor, but they are still very small. They are so small that 25,000 water droplets along the edge of your ruler would reach only to the one-inch mark.

Do clouds freeze in cold weather?

Yes, the water vapor and the water droplets of a cloud can turn to ice crystals, when the cloud is very cold.

Is fog a cloud that has come down from the sky?

No. Fog is a cloud that was formed right on the ground to begin with, or on a river or a lake, or on the sea.

Whenever water vapor is cooled, it turns into water droplets. When this happens in the sky, we have clouds. When it happens on the ground, we have fog.

How is water vapor cooled near the ground? It is cooled when air holding water vapor moves across cool earth or across a cool river or lake. Sometimes water vapor is cooled when it floats off from a wet, warm surface into cool air.

Fog is made in other ways, too, but all fogs start down on the level of the ground or of a body of water.

What makes a fog go away?

Sometimes the wind blows a fog away from where you are, and then it is foggy someplace else. But usually the air gets warmer, because of a warm wind or because the sun shines on it. Then the water droplets of the fog change back to water vapor again. Since you can't *see* water vapor — no more fog!

What is the difference between fog and smog?

Sometimes chimneys or automobiles or forest fires pour a great deal of smoke into the air. If the air is already foggy, the smoke mixes with the fog and becomes smog.

FAIR TODAY, BUT RAIN TOMORROW

What makes the rain come down from the clouds?

One part of a cloud is sometimes cooler than another part. This makes the different parts of a cloud move around. Then the water droplets of the cloud bump and push against each other.

When the droplets touch, they join together and make larger droplets.

When the larger droplets become too large and too heavy to float in the air, they begin to fall. As they fall, they often pick up more small droplets that they pass. Then they grow still larger, and still heavier, and fall even faster. . . . And then it's time for you to open your umbrella.

How big are little raindrops? How big are big ones?

You would have to put a hundred very little raindrops side by side to make a line of them just one inch long.

But the really big raindrops, the kind that go *splat!* when they hit the sidewalk, are about as big as green peas. When raindrops start to grow bigger than that, the air rushing past them as they fall usually breaks them apart into smaller drops again.

Why does it get dark before it rains?

A raincloud has come between you and the sun, and the sun's light doesn't reach the part of the earth where you are. You are standing in the cloud's shadow.

Sometimes you see the sun shining while it is raining. Why?

Suppose the rain is coming down from a small rain-cloud right above you. And the sun is off to the side in a part of the sky where there isn't any cloud. Then the sun can shine on you from off to the side, even while it's raining on you from straight overhead.

What is a rainbow? Where do the colors come from?

We say that ordinary sunlight is white light, but it is really many colors of light mixed together. Rays of light often bend when they pass from air into water, or from water into air. When rays of white sunlight bend in certain ways, all the different mixed colors of the sunlight spread apart, and you can see each color by itself.

Suppose the sun is shining while it is raining. The sun's light passes through the raindrops. If you are standing in just the right place, you may see a striped band of all the different colors of the sunlight curving across the sky. This is a rainbow.

When you see a rainbow, you are looking at sunlight after it has been spread apart by thousands and millions of falling raindrops.

Why are there sometimes weeks and weeks when it doesn't rain?

Several different things have to happen to make it rain at any one place. If they don't all happen at the same time, or in the right order, then it doesn't rain there.

Sometimes the upper air stays warm for a while, so that the water vapor in it doesn't cool off and turn to water droplets. Then no rainclouds form at all.

Or there might be times when the wind keeps blowing the water vapor away, so that it forms clouds somewhere else.

Or perhaps rainclouds do form, but a wind carries the clouds away before their water droplets get heavy enough to fall as rain.

Or sometimes rainclouds bump into a mountain. As soon as the clouds touch the mountain, they empty all their rain but only on one side of the mountain! The clouds never get past the mountain at all, and so it doesn't rain on the other side.

These are some of the reasons why it may not rain for weeks and weeks.

Does dew come down from the sky like rain?

No, dew doesn't come down from anywhere; dew is made right where you find it.

Dew comes from water vapor in the air, during a clear, cool night with no wind.

When the sun sets, the ground usually grows cooler. Then the cool ground cools the warm, damp air just above it. But the cooled air can not hold as much water vapor as the warm air could. So the water vapor in the cooled air turns to tiny drops of water. These tiny water drops cling to blades of grass and to leaves and flowers and to almost anything else cool that the warmer air touches.

SNOWFLAKES AND SLEET, HAILSTONES AND FROST

Snowflakes weigh hardly anything. Why do they fall to the ground?

It is true that one snowflake doesn't weigh very much. But it weighs more than the same amount of air would weigh. Snow is heavier than air, and so it falls through the air to the earth.

Where is snow made?

Snow is made exactly where rain is made — in the clouds. When it is very cold in the clouds, the water vapor and the water droplets freeze into crystals of ice. These crystals fall the way raindrops fall, when they get heavy enough.

Are all snowflakes shaped like stars?

No. Sometimes water vapor and water droplets freeze into crystals shaped like flat stars, but sometimes the crystals have other shapes. And even the star-shaped crystals often break as they fall, or change their shapes before they reach the earth.

The next time it snows, hold out your arm and see how many tiny stars you can find on the sleeve of your coat.

Some snow is like hard sand hitting you, and some snow is like feathers. Why?

As snow falls, the crystals may bang together and break, or they may stick together and tangle, or they may fall through separate layers of warm and cold air so that they melt a little and then freeze again into different shapes.

Sometimes the ice crystals pack together tightly into small, hard, white grains. And sometimes they cling together in big, fluffy, feathery clumps. It all depends on what happens to them, and what kind of air they pass through, on their way down from the clouds to the earth.

What is the difference between sleet and snow?

Snow is water vapor and water droplets that have frozen into six-sided *crystals* of ice.

Sleet is raindrops, or sometimes melted snowflakes, that have frozen into little, hard, heavy *lumps* of ice. Sleet bounces when it hits the ground, and it hurts when it blows against your face.

What are hailstones?

Hail is made when different kinds of up-and-down and warm-and-cold winds blow all around and inside a special kind of raincloud.

A raindrop begins to fall from the cloud, and then it is blown up to where the air is cold and it freezes into a small lump of ice. Then it comes down again and half melts. Then it falls through another layer of cold air, or else it is swirled up again into cold air, and it freezes once more.

It melts and freezes and melts and freezes, and by the time it hits the ground it may be a ball of ice in layers, like a little icy onion, or it may be a rough chunk of ice with no special shape at all. Hailstones are made most often during summer thunderstorms.

HAILSTONES

What is frost? Where does it come from?

Frost comes from water vapor in the air, just as dew does, and for the same reason. (Dew is explained on page 37.) But frost forms only when the temperature of the ground is freezing (32 degrees Fahrenheit) or lower. When the freezing ground chills the air above it, the water vapor in the air freezes into tiny ice crystals. These crystals make a sparkling white coat of frost on twigs and leaves and stones and on the ground itself.

FLASH AND CRASH

Why is lightning sometimes a zigzag and sometimes only a flash?

Lightning is really not zigzag, the way drawings so often show it. It usually travels in a wiggly sort of line.

Not this   but this   or this

If you are not looking at the lightning itself, or if it is too far away for you to see, then all you see is a flash. This flash is the light of the lightning stroke, shining against the clouds or against the rain that is falling.

How fast is lightning?

Very fast — as fast as lightning!
If a stroke of lightning could travel along the equator, it would go all the way around the earth in just a little more than one second.

What is thunder?

Thunder is the sound that lightning makes. You could say that a lightning stroke makes a path for itself by exploding the air it passes through. The air around the lightning's path gets pushed back in waves, very suddenly and very hard. It is the sound of these air waves being pushed that we call thunder.

Which comes first, lightning or thunder?

Neither — the flash and the crash happen at the same time. But light travels much more quickly than sound. If there is a stroke of lightning two miles away, you *see* it the instant it flashes. But you won't *hear* it until about ten seconds later.

YOU AND I AND THE WEATHER FORECASTER

Can we make it rain? Can we make it stop raining?

All through history, people have tried to make it rain. Native Americans danced rain dances; other people prayed to their gods; still others used charms, or sang special rain songs.

Today, we still try to make it rain. We can't do it every time we try. And we can't do it everywhere. And we can't make it rain very much. But we can do it sometimes, and in some places, and a little.

Airplanes fly over or through certain kinds of rain-clouds, and "seed" them with dry ice and chemicals. If the clouds and the wind and the temperature and several other things are just right, down comes the rain.

There must be many people who would like to find a way to make it stop raining too. But no one has ever been able to do that, so far.

How do forecasters predict weather? How do they know what it's going to be like tomorrow?

Weather forecasters don't usually know *exactly* what tomorrow's weather will be, but they have a pretty good idea.

There are weather instruments of all kinds all over the earth today. There are balloons and kites carrying weather instruments high above the earth, too. These instruments can measure the speed and direction of the wind, the amount of water vapor in the air, and the temperature.

By using radio and telegraph, forecasters in one part of the world can always find out just what is going on in every other part of the world.

A forecaster knows, for example, when cold air is blowing toward us, even when it's a thousand miles away. He knows how fast it is moving. He knows when there are other winds, perhaps warmer ones, blowing somewhere else. He knows if the warm wind is likely to meet the cold air and mix with it, or push it off in another direction. And he knows when and where this is likely to happen.

ISBN 0-590-41142-X

Text copyright © 1969 by M. Jean Craig.
Illustrations copyright © 1996 by Scholastic Inc.
All rights reserved. Published by Scholastic Inc.

12 11 10 9 8 7 6   9/9 0 1/0

Printed in the U.S.A.   23

First Scholastic printing, March 1996

Book design by Laurie Williams